Step-by-Step
TRANSPARENT ART

JOAN WHITEHEAD

Step-by-Step
TRANSPARENT ART

JOAN WHITEHEAD

GUILD OF MASTER CRAFTSMAN PUBLICATIONS

First published 2007 by
Guild of Master Craftsman Publications Ltd
166 High Street, Lewes
East Sussex, BN7 1XU

ISBN 978-1-86108-504-7

British Cataloguing in Publication Data
A catalogue record of this book is available from the British Library.

Managing Editor: Gerrie Purcell
Production Manager: Jim Bulley
Editor: Rachel Netherwood
Managing Art Editor: Gilda Pacitti
Designer: James Hollywell

Typefaces: BellCent & Dearjoe
Colour reproduction by AltaImage
Printed and bound by Hing Yip Printing Company Limited.

CONTENTS

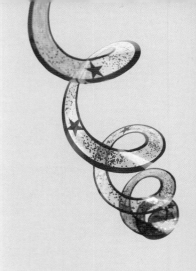

PROJECTS

ABOUT THE AUTHOR

Joan Whitehead was born and grew up in the UK. Her love of art led her to study at Bolton College of Art. She now lives in Denmark, Western Australia, where she runs a private art gallery selling a variety of media, including her transparent art designs. Her work has featured in exhibitions all over Australia.

INTRODUCTION

After several years of working with glass – designing and making lead lights and sun catchers – it was a natural progression into working with plastic, which is a much easier medium with which to work. I used several of my glass sun catcher designs for my first transparent art projects but, like everything I seem to do, the plastic art work snowballed and soon took over from the glass.

The use of the glitter, sprinkling it on while the paint

is still wet, creates a lovely effect. It adds a touch of sparkle and can also eliminate any poor brush work, giving a smooth, professional finish.

All the designs in this book are for sale in my gallery. After being asked hundreds of times how I

make different things, I decided to share my designs and the know-how so that you can have the pleasure of creating transparent art yourself. The projects are so versatile they can be used for all sorts of things, from sun catchers to decorations. They can even be used to embellish greetings cards. Being made from clear plastic there is no need to be very exact in cutting the projects out. So they are easy to create – making them perfect for all ages and skill levels.

Materials

Double-sided
sticky tape

Hammer

Transparent glass paint

Wire

Stapler
(size 10 staples)

A pair of sharp
craft scissors

Medium tip black
marker pen

Fine craft glitter

It is useful to have
turps, for cleaning
your brushes. You
will also need
access to a
photocopier.

Watercolour paintbrush

Transparent acetate sheets

BUTTERFLY 1

Make a kaleidoscope of butterflies in
bright and beautiful colours.

You will need...

- Transparent photocopy sheet
- Double-sided sticky tape
- Paint: yellow
- Paintbrush
- Glitter: red and silver
- Stapler and size 10 staples
- Hammer
- Black felt-tip pen

Tip

I find it easier to colour the tops of the staples black before putting them in the stapler.

▼ The finished design

1 Photocopy Butterfly 1 onto a transparent photocopy sheet (see page 68). Apply yellow transparency colour to the wings. Allow to dry.

2 Paint on dots and dashes using yellow paint. Apply red glitter while the paint is still wet. Allow to dry, shake off excess glitter and cut out.

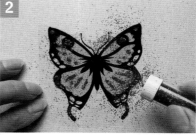

3 Staple the top wing to the body and wing piece using two size 10 staples. Turn the butterfly over, and hammer the staples flat.

4 Apply double-sided sticky tape to the back, then turn over and colour the front of the staples with the black felt-tip pen.

5 Fold the top wings up to create a 3D effect. Paint the body and apply silver glitter, while still wet, to finish off. Shake off any excess glitter.

The template used

RAIN BIRD

This cheeky little fellow on his perch will really lift
your spirits on a grey and soggy day.

You will need...

- Transparent photocopy sheet
- Double-sided sticky tape
- Paint: red, blue, green, yellow and turquoise
- Paintbrush
- Glitter: red, blue, green, gold and silver

Tip

A sharp tap on the edge of the plastic helps to remove the excess glitter.

▼ The finished design

1 Photocopy the rain bird pattern (see page 68) onto a transparent photocopy sheet and cut out around the outside edge. Affix double-sided sticky tape to the back.

2 Paint two stripes on the umbrella red and sprinkle with red glitter while still wet. Allow to dry and shake off any excess glitter.

3 Apply green paint to the body of the bird and sprinkle with green glitter while still wet. Allow to dry. Shake off any excess glitter.

4 Paint the other stripes on the umbrella blue and sprinkle with blue glitter while still wet. Allow to dry. Shake off excess glitter.

5 Paint the beak and branch yellow, adding gold glitter. Allow to dry. Paint the frame turquoise, add silver glitter and allow to dry. Shake off any excess glitter.

The template used

MOSAIC

This elegant, Art Deco-inspired design will look fantastic
displayed in a hallway like a piece of stained glass.

You will need...

- Transparent photocopy sheet
- Double-sided sticky tape
- Paint: yellow, blue, red and orange
- Paintbrush
- Glitter: gold, silver and red

1 Photocopy the mosaic pattern (see page 69) onto a transparent photocopy sheet. Cut out around the outside edge of the main pattern and small flowers.

2 Apply yellow paint and sprinkle with gold glitter. Allow to dry. Fix double-sided tape to the back of the main pattern and the flowers.

3 Apply blue paint as shown and sprinkle with silver glitter while still wet. Allow to dry and then shake off any excess glitter.

4 Paint the flowers red and sprinkle with red glitter. Paint the border orange and add gold glitter. Allow to dry. Shake off any excess glitter.

5 Stick the small flowers to the front of the main pattern and fold the petals up. Add silver glitter to the centre of the flowers to finish off.

▼ The finished design

The template used

RAINBOW SPIRAL

Make lots of these fun spirals in different colours
and display them together for a great effect.

You will need...

- Transparent photocopy sheet
- Double-sided sticky tape
- Paint: as many colours as you like
- Paintbrush
- Glitter: gold
- Cotton thread
- Small weight – such as a coloured plastic bead

Tip

Using the same glitter throughout this project helps to tie all the colours together, creating a lovely effect.

▼ The finished design

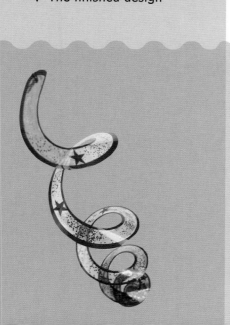

1 Photocopy the rainbow spiral pattern onto a transparent photocopy sheet (see page 69). Then cut around the outside edge of the spiral.

2 Using as many colours as you like, colour the spiral to each star motif. While still wet, add gold glitter and allow to dry. Shake off excess glitter.

3 Carefully cut down the middle of the black line into the centre.

4 Make a hole at the outside of the spiral and thread some cotton through to make a loop for hanging.

5 Using double-sided sticky tape, attach the small weight on the bottom of the swirl and then hang it up!

The template used

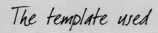

DAISIES

The daisies in this cheerful design are sure to inspire feelings of warm, sunny days.

You will need...

- Transparent photocopy sheet
- Double-sided sticky tape
- Paint: yellow, pink, orange and light green
- Paintbrush
- Glitter: silver and gold

1 Photocopy the daisies onto a transparent sheet (see page 70). Paint the centres yellow. Sprinkle with gold glitter, allow to dry and shake off any excess glitter.

2 Colour the petals with pink paint and sprinkle with silver glitter while still wet. Allow to dry and shake off any excess glitter.

3 Colour the flower with orange paint and sprinkle with gold glitter while still wet. Allow to dry and shake off excess glitter.

4 Paint the background light green. Sprinkle with silver glitter while still wet. Allow to dry. Shake off any excess.

5 Attach double-sided tape to the back. Cut out the small flower and attach to the left-hand flower with double-sided tape. Fold the petals up.

▼ The finished design

The template used

PARROT

Give your home a flavour of tropical rainforest life
with this striking parrot design.

You will need...

- Transparent photocopy sheet
- Double-sided sticky tape
- Paint: red, orange, pale blue and yellow
- Paintbrush
- Glitter: red, gold, blue and silver

1 Photocopy the parrot pattern (see page 70) onto a transparent photocopy sheet. Cut out around the outside edge and apply double-sided tape to the back.

2 Paint the head and neck red. Sprinkle with red glitter while still wet. Allow to dry and then shake off any excess glitter.

3 Paint the tree branch orange and sprinkle with gold glitter while still wet. Allow to dry and shake off the excess glitter.

4 Apply pale blue paint to the parrot's wings and tail. Sprinkle with blue glitter while still wet. Allow to dry and shake off any excess glitter.

5 Turn the design over and paint the bird's chest and the frame yellow. Add gold glitter to the bird and silver glitter to the frame. Allow to dry. Shake off excess glitter.

▼ The finished design

The template used

FROG 1

Any little nature fans will love to see a jumping
green frog on their bedroom window.

You will need...

- Transparent photocopy sheet
- Double-sided sticky tape
- Paint: green, yellow and red
- Paintbrush
- Glitter: green, gold and red

1 Photocopy the pattern of frog number 1 (see page 70) onto a transparent photocopy sheet and cut out.

2 Affix a piece of double-sided sticky tape to the back of the frog.

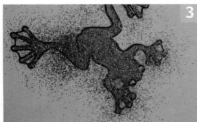

3 Apply green paint to the main body of the frog. While still wet, sprinkle on the green glitter. Allow to dry and shake off any excess.

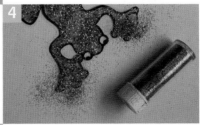

4 Apply yellow paint to the webs between the toes. While still wet, sprinkle on the gold glitter. Allow to dry and shake off any excess.

5 Apply red paint to the eyes and sprinkle on the red glitter while still wet. Allow to dry and shake off any excess.

▼ The finished design

The template used

FAIRY 1

Add a sprinkling of fairy magic with this
delicately dancing figure of fantasy.

You will need...

- Transparent photocopy sheet
- Double-sided sticky tape
- Paint: orange, blue, yellow, purple and pink
- Paintbrush
- Glitter: gold, blue and silver

1 Photocopy the pattern of fairy number 1 (see page 71) onto a transparent photocopy sheet and cut out. Apply double-sided sticky tape to the back of the fairy.

2 Paint the hair orange and sprinkle with gold glitter while still wet. Allow to dry. Paint the dress top blue and sprinkle with blue glitter while still wet. Allow to dry and shake off any excess glitter.

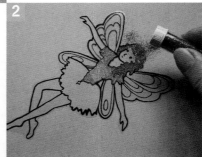

3 Apply yellow paint to the wings and sprinkle with gold glitter while still wet. Paint the skirt purple and sprinkle with silver glitter while still wet. Allow to dry. Shake off any excess glitter.

4 Apply pink paint to the arms, legs and face. Allow to dry before handling.

▼ The finished design

The template used

BUTTERFLY 2

This design was inspired by a Red Admiral butterfly,
but you don't just have to paint it red!

You will need...

- Transparent photocopy sheet
- Double-sided sticky tape
- Paint: pink
- Paintbrush
- Glitter: silver
- Stapler and size 10 staples
- Hammer
- Black felt-tip pen

1 Photocopy the pattern of butterfly 2 onto a transparent photocopy sheet (see page 71). Paint the wings pink as shown and allow to dry.

2 Paint on dots and dashes in pink. Add silver glitter while still wet. Allow to dry and shake off any excess glitter. Then cut out as shown.

3 Staple the top wing to the body and wing piece using two size 10 staples.

4 Turn the butterfly over, and hammer the staples flat. Attach double-sided tape and colour the front of the staples with the black felt-tip.

5 Finally, fold the top wings up and your butterfly is ready to fly away.

▼ The finished design

The template used

BLUE BIRD

With his dark blue tail and vibrant turquoise wings,
this Blue Bird is set to soar.

You will need...

- Transparent photocopy sheet
- Double-sided sticky tape
- Paint: dark blue and light blue
- Paintbrush
- Glitter: blue and silver
- Stapler and size 10 staples
- Hammer
- Black felt-tip pen

1 Photocopy the blue bird pattern onto a transparent photocopy sheet (see page 71). Carefully cut the shape out.

2 Apply dark blue paint as shown. Sprinkle with blue glitter while the paint is still wet and allow to dry. Shake off any excess glitter.

3 Apply light blue paint to the wings and sprinkle with silver glitter while still wet. Allow to dry and shake off excess glitter.

4 Staple the top wings to the main body using two size 10 staples. Turn over to the back and hammer the staples flat. Attach the double-sided tape.

5 Apply some black felt-tip pen to the front of the staples and fold the top wings up to create a 3D effect.

▼ The finished design, showing a colour variation

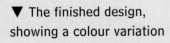
The template used

DRAGONS

Fearsome and fiery – these fantastical creatures
will make a bold statement in any setting.

You will need...

- Transparent photocopy sheet
- Double-sided sticky tape
- Paint: red, green, yellow, blue and turquoise
- Paintbrush
- Glitter: red, green, gold, blue and silver

1 Photocopy the dragon pattern (see page 72) onto a transparent photocopy sheet and cut out around the outside edge. Apply double-sided sticky tape to the back.

2 Apply red paint to the wings on one dragon and to the flame on the other. Sprinkle with red glitter while still wet and allow to dry. Shake off any excess glitter.

3 Apply green paint as shown and sprinkle with green glitter while still wet. Allow to dry and shake off excess glitter.

4 Apply yellow paint as shown. Sprinkle with gold glitter while still wet. Allow to dry and shake off any excess glitter.

5 Apply blue paint as shown. Add blue glitter while still wet. Allow to dry. Paint the frame turquoise, add silver glitter and allow to dry. Shake off excess glitter.

▼ The finished design

The template used

FLOWER

Pick a bunch of delicate, tropical blooms in summery shades of orange and pink.

You will need...

- Transparent photocopy sheet
- Double-sided sticky tape
- Paint: yellow, turquoise and pink
- Paintbrush
- Stapler and size 10 staples
- Hammer
- Glitter: silver

Tip

Add the flower to your gift wrapping, to give a special present that personal touch.

▼ The finished design

1 Photocopy the pattern of the flower (see page 72) onto a transparent photocopy sheet. Cut it out, right down to the outside of the centre of the flower.

2 Paint the leaves yellow and turquoise and the petals pink. Add silver glitter while still wet. Allow to dry and shake off any excess glitter.

3 Place the small petals on top of the large petals and leaves. Staple all the pieces together in the centre of the flower.

4 Turn over and hammer the staples flat before applying double-sided sticky tape. Turn back over and fold up the top petals to create a 3D effect.

5 Finish off by painting the centre of the flower pink. Add silver glitter while still wet. Allow to dry and shake off any excess.

The template used

BLUE WREN

Wildlife watchers will love this feathery friend
with its jaunty stance, about to take flight.

You will need...

- Transparent photocopy sheet
- Double-sided sticky tape
- Paint: dark blue, light blue, brown, green and turquoise
- Paintbrush
- Stapler and size 10 staples
- Hammer
- Glitter: blue, silver, gold and green

1 Photocopy the blue wren pattern (see page 72) onto a transparent photocopy sheet and cut out around the outside edge. Affix double-sided sticky tape to the back.

2 Paint the bird dark blue and add blue glitter. Paint under the eye light blue and add silver glitter. Allow to dry. Shake off any excess glitter.

3 Apply brown paint to the branch and gum nuts and sprinkle with gold glitter while still wet. Allow to dry and shake off excess glitter.

4 Apply green paint to the leaves, sprinkling with green glitter while still wet. Allow to dry and shake off the excess glitter.

5 Turn over and apply turquoise paint to the oval frame. Sprinkle with silver glitter while still wet. Allow to dry and then shake off any excess glitter.

▼ The finished design, showing a colour variation

The template used

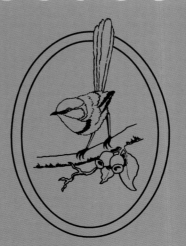

BUTTERFLY 3

This striking butterfly is vibrant in eye-catching
colours of turquoise and silver.

34

You will need...

- Transparent photocopy sheet
- Paint: turquoise
- Paintbrush
- Stapler and size 10 staples
- Hammer
- Glitter: silver
- Black felt-tip pen
- Wire

Tip

This butterfly looks lovely placed in a plant pot or flower arrangement.

▼ The finished design

1 Photocopy butterfly 3 (see page 73) onto a transparent photocopy sheet. Apply turquoise paint to the wings and allow to dry.

2 Paint turquoise dots and dashes on the wings. Add silver glitter while still wet and allow to dry. Shake off any excess glitter and cut out.

3 Staple the top wing to the body and wing piece using two size 10 staples.

4 Turn the butterfly over, and thread the wire under the staples. Apply black felt pen to the front of the staples.

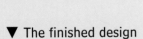

5 Finally, bend the wire down and fold the top wings up, as shown.

The template used

BUMBLEBEE

Busy yourself with this cheerful design.
Why not create a swarm of dancing bumblebees?

1 Photocopy the bumblebee pattern (see page 73) onto a transparent photocopy sheet. Cut out around the outside edge and inside the dotted line.

You will need...

- Transparent photocopy sheet
- Double-sided sticky tape
- Paint: yellow, orange and red
- Paintbrush
- Stapler and size 10 staples
- Hammer
- Glitter: silver, gold and red
- Black felt-tip pen

2 Colour the wings and eye in yellow paint and sprinkle with silver glitter while still wet. Allow to dry and shake off any excess glitter.

3 Colour the body orange and sprinkle with gold glitter while still wet. Allow to dry. Paint the head red. Add red glitter and allow to dry. Shake off the excess glitter.

4 Staple the top wing to the body using two size 10 staples. Turn the bee over and hammer the staples flat. Affix double-sided sticky tape.

5 Turn the bee back over and colour the tops of the staples with the felt-tip. Fold the wings up to create the 3D effect.

▼ The finished design

The template used

ROUND FLOWERS

A kaleidescope of dazzling colours complements this
delightful floral display.

You will need...

- Transparent photocopy sheet
- Double-sided sticky tape
- Paint: yellow, green, red, orange, light blue, dark blue and purple
- Paintbrush
- Glitter: gold, green, red and silver

1 Photocopy the round pattern (see page 73) onto a transparent photocopy sheet and cut out around outside edge. Apply double-sided sticky tape to the back.

2 Apply yellow and green paint as shown. Sprinkle, while still wet, with gold and green glitter. Allow to dry and shake off any excess glitter.

3 Apply red and orange paint as shown. While still wet, sprinkle with red and gold glitter and allow to dry. Shake off any excess glitter.

4 Add the light blue and dark blue colours and sprinkle with silver glitter while still wet. Allow to dry. Shake off any excess glitter.

5 Turn over and apply purple paint to the outer circle. While still wet sprinkle with silver glitter. Allow to dry and shake off any excess glitter.

▼ The finished design

The template used

FLYING DUCK

A new twist on the traditional three flying ducks,
this project will definitely attract attention.

1 Photocopy the pattern of the duck (see page 74) onto a transparent photocopy sheet and cut out around the outside edge. Affix double-sided sticky tape to the back.

You will need...

- Transparent photocopy sheet
- Double-sided sticky tape
- Paint: yellow, orange, green, light blue and dark blue
- Paintbrush
- Glitter: gold, green, silver and blue

2 Apply yellow paint and sprinkle with gold glitter, while still wet, as shown. Allow to dry and shake off any excess glitter.

3 Paint the wings and the tail orange. Sprinkle with gold glitter while still wet and allow to dry. Then shake off any excess glitter.

4 Colour the grass and the duck's neck with green paint and sprinkle with green glitter while still wet. Allow to dry and shake off any excess glitter.

5 Paint the water pale blue and sprinkle with silver glitter. Allow to dry. Turn over and paint the frame dark blue. Add blue glitter, allow to dry and shake off excess glitter.

▼ The finished design

The template used

FAIRY 2

Any little girl would be delighted to have a fairy
on her bedroom mirror or window.

You will need...

- Transparent photocopy sheet
- Double-sided sticky tape
- Paint: yellow, green, purple, orange and pink
- Paintbrush
- Glitter: silver, green and gold

1 Photocopy the pattern of fairy 2 (see page 74) onto a transparent photocopy sheet and cut out. Fix double-sided sticky tape to the back.

2 Paint the hair yellow and add silver glitter while still wet. Allow to dry, then paint the dress top green and add green glitter. Allow to dry and shake off any excess glitter.

3 Apply purple paint to the wings and add silver glitter. Allow to dry. Paint the skirt orange and sprinkle with gold glitter. Allow to dry and shake off any excess glitter.

4 Apply pink paint to the arms, legs and face. Allow to dry before handling.

▼ The finished design

The template used

FISH

Go overboard to create a miniature water world
complete with tropical fish.

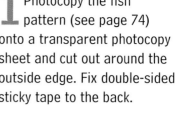

You will need...

- Transparent photocopy sheet
- Double-sided sticky tape
- Paint: yellow, orange, green and pale blue
- Paintbrush
- Glitter: gold, green and silver

1 Photocopy the fish pattern (see page 74) onto a transparent photocopy sheet and cut out around the outside edge. Fix double-sided sticky tape to the back.

2 Colour the top fish with yellow paint. Sprinkle with gold glitter while wet. Allow to dry and shake off any excess glitter.

3 Apply orange paint to the bottom fish and sprinkle with gold glitter while still wet. Allow to dry. Shake off any excess glitter.

4 Paint the seaweed green. While the paint is still wet, sprinkle with green glitter. Allow to dry and shake off any excess glitter.

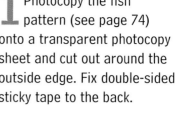

5 Apply pale blue paint to the background. Sprinkle with silver glitter and allow to dry. Shake off any excess glitter.

▼ The finished design

The template used

FROG 2

This grinning, green frog is guaranteed to cheer up
any dull corners of your home.

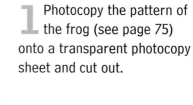

You will need...

- Transparent photocopy sheet
- Double-sided sticky tape
- Paint: green, red and yellow
- Paintbrush
- Glitter: green and gold

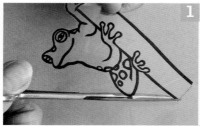

1 Photocopy the pattern of the frog (see page 75) onto a transparent photocopy sheet and cut out.

2 Affix double-sided sticky tape to the back.

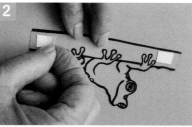

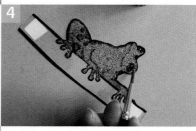

3 Apply green colour to the frog. While still wet, sprinkle on green glitter and allow to dry. Shake off any excess glitter.

4 Apply red colour to the small circles and around the eyes. Allow to dry.

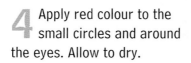

5 Paint the tree yellow and sprinkle on gold glitter while the paint is still wet. Allow to dry and shake off any excess glitter.

▼ The finished design

The template used

DRAGONFLY

Decorate little glass candle jars with colourful dragonflies and use them to decorate a table.

You will need...

- Transparent photocopy sheet
- Double-sided sticky tape
- Paint: yellow, blue and red
- Paintbrush
- Glitter: gold, blue and red
- Stapler and size 10 staples
- Hammer
- Black felt-tip pen

1 Photocopy the pattern (see page 75) onto a transparent sheet. Cut out. Paint the body yellow, add gold glitter and allow to dry. Shake off excess glitter.

2 Paint the wings blue. Add blue glitter. Paint the eyes red and add red glitter. Allow to dry between colours and shake off excess glitter.

3 Staple the top wing onto the full body piece with two size 10 staples. Turn the dragonfly over and hammer the staples flat.

4 Attach double-sided sticky tape to the back. Turn back over and colour the front of the staples with the black pen.

5 Fold the top wings up to create the 3D effect.

▼ The finished design

The template used

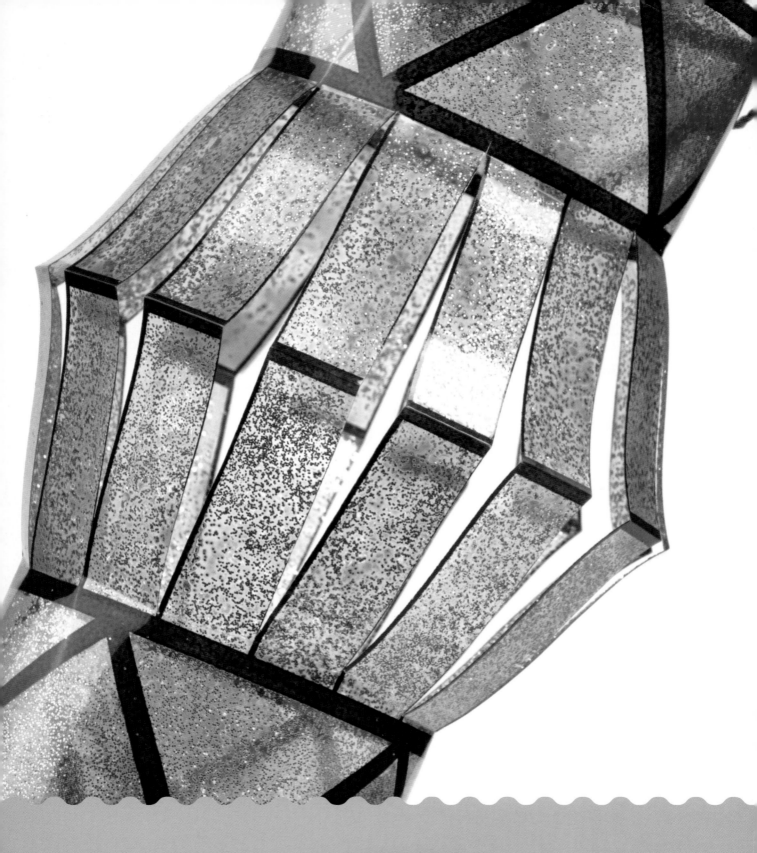

LANTERN

Make lanterns in different colours and hang them up in the trees
for a spectacular summer display.

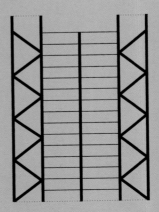

You will need...

- Transparent photocopy sheet
- Double-sided sticky tape
- Paint: yellow, orange and turquoise
- Paintbrush
- Glitter: silver
- Stapler and size 10 staples
- Hammer
- Black felt-tip pen
- Cord

Tip

Folding the plastic against a steel rule will make the process much easier.

▼ The finished design

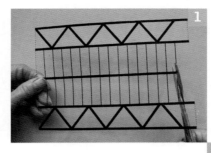

1 Photocopy the pattern of the lantern (see page 75) onto a transparent photocopy sheet. Cut out around the outside edge and along the dotted lines.

2 Allowing to dry between colours, paint the lantern yellow, orange and turquoise. Add glitter while still wet and shake off any excess.

3 Fold the lantern along the centre line, and then fold in the edges as shown.

4 Holding the lantern firmly, cut from the centre fold along each of the lines down to the other two folds.

5 Bend the lantern round and fasten with tape to hold in place while stapling. Use two size 10 staples at each end. Make two holes and thread the cord for hanging.

The template used

51

SPIDER AND WEB

Not one for arachnophobes. This big spider in its
colourful web isn't so spooky, is it?

You will need...

- Transparent photocopy sheet
- Double-sided sticky tape
- Paint: red, turquoise, yellow and blue
- Paintbrush
- Glitter: red and silver

1 Photocopy the pattern of the spider and web (see page 76) onto a transparent photocopy sheet and cut out.

2 Attach double-sided sticky tape to the back.

3 Paint the spider red and add red glitter. Allow to dry. Paint parts of the web red and add silver glitter. Shake off any excess glitter.

4 Add turquoise paint to more parts of the web and add silver glitter while still wet. Allow to dry and shake off any excess glitter.

5 Paint other areas of the web in yellow. Sprinkle with silver glitter while still wet and allow to dry. Shake off any excess glitter.

6 Finish off with some blue paint, adding silver glitter while still wet. Allow to dry. Shake off any excess glitter.

▼ The finished design

The template used

WITCH

Decorate the house at Hallowe'en with this purple witch
to add a little hocus pocus.

You will need...

- Transparent photocopy sheet
- Double-sided sticky tape
- Paint: yellow, orange, red, dark blue, purple, light blue and pink
- Paintbrush
- Glitter: gold, red, silver and purple

1 Photocopy the pattern of the witch (see page 76) onto a transparent photocopy sheet and cut out around the outside edge. Attach double-sided sticky tape to the back.

2 Paint the broom handle yellow and the bristles orange. Sprinkle the wet paint with gold glitter. Allow to dry. Shake off any excess.

3 Paint the hat trim red and add red glitter. Paint the hills dark blue. Add silver glitter and allow to dry. Shake off any excess glitter.

4 Paint the witch's coat with purple colour, sprinkling with purple glitter. Allow to dry and shake off the excess.

5 Paint the sky light blue. Sprinkle with silver glitter and once dry, shake off the excess glitter. Finally, paint the face and hands pink, and your witch is ready to fly.

▼ The finished design

The template used

CHRISTMAS TREE

Making this quick and easy decoration is ideal
to fit into the hectic run-up to the festive season.

You will need...

- Transparent photocopy sheet
- Double-sided sticky tape
- Paint: yellow, orange, green, light blue, dark blue and red
- Paintbrush
- Glitter: green and silver
- Stapler and size 10 staples
- Hammer
- Black felt-tip pen

1 Photocopy the pattern of the tree (see page 76) onto a transparent photocopy sheet and cut out. Attach double-sided sticky tape to the back of the main tree.

2 Paint the different sections of the tree green. While still wet sprinkle on green glitter and allow to dry. Shake off any excess glitter.

3 Paint the tinsel light blue and the rest of the tree with the other colours. Add silver glitter while still wet. Allow to dry between colours.

4 Staple the two decorated pieces onto the main tree using size 10 staples. Hammer the back of the staples flat. Colour the top staple black.

5 Finally, fold the two top pieces up to create a 3D effect and the tree is all set to sparkle!

▼ The finished design

The template used

ANGEL

So versatile at Christmas time, this stunning angel could sit on top of the tree, transform a greetings card and much more...

You will need...

- Transparent photocopy sheet
- Double-sided sticky tape
- Paint: yellow, pink and turquoise
- Paintbrush
- Glitter: silver

1 Photocopy the pattern of the angel (see page 77) onto a transparent photocopy sheet. Cut out around the outside edge and inside the dotted line.

2 Paint the wings yellow and pink as shown. Sprinkle silver glitter while the colour is still wet. Allow to dry and shake off the excess glitter.

3 Paint the angel pink, yellow and turquoise as shown, and add silver glitter. Allow to dry between colours. Shake off any excess glitter.

4 Paint the face and hands pink. Fix double-sided tape to the section within the dotted line on the angel's back. Fold the wings in half and attach.

5 Turn the angel over and attach the double-sided sticky tape in place.

▼ The finished design

The template used

HOLLY

One of the most enduring of all festive images, shiny holly and
bright red berries are a true Christmas classic.

60

You will need...

- Transparent photocopy sheet
- Double-sided sticky tape
- Paint: green and red
- Paintbrush
- Glitter: green and red
- Stapler and size 10 staples
- Hammer
- Black felt-tip pen

Tip

Attach a few of the holly leaves onto a cane or wire ring for a lovely Christmas wreath.

▼ The finished design

1 Photocopy the holly pattern (see page 77) onto a transparent photocopy sheet, and cut out around the outside edge and along the dotted line.

2 Paint the leaves green. Add green glitter and allow to dry. Paint the berries red and add red glitter. Allow to dry. Shake off excess glitter.

3 Staple the top leaf and berry piece onto the bottom leaves piece, using three size 10 staples.

4 Turn over and hammer the staples flat. Attach double-sided sticky tape. Turn it over to the right side and colour the top of the staples black.

5 Fold the top leaves up to create a 3D effect. You could add string and hang these on your Christmas tree.

The template used

SNOWMAN

This friendly snowman decoration will never melt away –
letting you enjoy it year after year.

You will need...

- Transparent photocopy sheet
- Double-sided sticky tape
- Paint: green, dark blue, red, orange and pale blue
- Paintbrush
- Glitter: white frosted

Tip

Staple a loop of cord onto the snowman's hat, using a size 10 staple, to make a delightful Christmas tree decoration.

1 Photocopy the snowman (see page 77) onto a transparent photocopy sheet. Cut out around the edge and inside the dotted line.

2 Paint the scarf green and the hat band dark blue. Allow to dry for a few minutes.

3 Paint the bird red and the carrot orange. Allow to dry.

4 Paint the main part of the snowman pale blue. Add white frosted glitter. Allow to dry. Shake off excess glitter.

5 Turn the snowman over and attach double-sided sticky tape.

▼ The finished design

The template used

BELLS

Nothing is more joyful than the sound of Christmas bells.
Capture that feeling in your home with this delightful design.

You will need...

 Transparent photocopy sheet
- Double-sided sticky tape
- Paint: green and yellow
- Paintbrush
- Glitter: green and gold
- Stapler and size 10 staples
- Hammer
- Black felt-tip pen

Tip

These bells will add a special touch to a festive parcel.

▼ The finished design

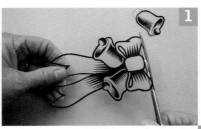

1 Photocopy the pattern of the bells (see page 78) onto a transparent photocopy sheet and cut out.

2 Paint the ribbon green and while still wet sprinkle on green glitter. Allow to dry and shake off any excess glitter.

3 Paint the bells yellow and sprinkle with gold glitter while still wet. Allow to dry and shake off any excess glitter.

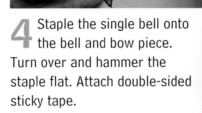

4 Staple the single bell onto the bell and bow piece. Turn over and hammer the staple flat. Attach double-sided sticky tape.

5 Turn back over and colour the top of the staple black. Fold up the top bell to create a 3D effect.

The template used

CANDLE

Enjoy the glow of candlelight without ever having to blow it out with this lovely festive project.

You will need...

- Transparent photocopy sheet
- Double-sided sticky tape
- Paint: red, yellow and green
- Paintbrush
- Glitter: red, gold and green
- Stapler and size 10 staples
- Hammer
- Black felt-tip pen

1 Photocopy the pattern of the candle (see page 78) onto a transparent photocopy sheet, and cut out around the outside edge. Attach double-sided sticky tape to the back.

2 Paint the candle and berries red and while still wet, sprinkle on red glitter. Allow to dry. Paint the outside of the flame yellow and add gold glitter. Allow to dry and shake off any excess glitter.

3 Paint the leaves green and sprinkle with green glitter while still wet. Allow to dry and shake off any excess glitter. Staple the top leaf and berries onto the bottom leaf.

4 Turn over to the back and hammer the staple flat. Attach double-sided tape. Turn back over and colour the front of the staple black. Fold up the top leaves.

▼ The finished design

The template used

TEMPLATES

All at 50%

BUTTERFLY 1

RAIN BIRD

MOSAIC

RAINBOW SPIRAL

DAISIES

PARROT

FROG 1

FAIRY 1

BUTTERFLY 2

BLUE BIRD

DRAGONS

FLOWER

BLUE WREN

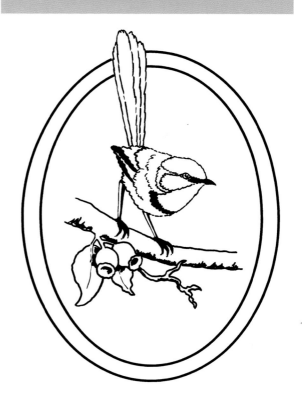

72

BUTTERFLY 3

BUMBLEBEE

ROUND FLOWERS

FLYING DUCK

FAIRY 2

FISH

74

FROG 2

DRAGONFLY

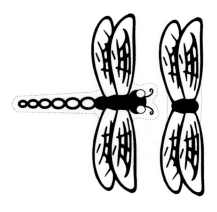

LANTERNS

SPIDER AND WEB

WITCH

CHRISTMAS TREE

ANGEL

HOLLY

SNOWMAN

BELLS

CANDLE

ACKNOWLEDGEMENTS

My appreciation goes to my family for their help and support.
Without their encouragement this book would not have been possible.

USEFUL ADDRESSES

Australia

Art Warehouse
PO Box 3650
Weston Creek
Canberra
ACT 2611
Tel: 1300 766 046
www.artwarehouse.com.au

Australian Craft Network Pty Ltd
PO Box 350
Narellan
NSW 2567
Tel: 62 107 869 879
www.auscraftnet.com.au

Little Packs Distribution
PO Box 1571
Bibra Lake
DC
Western Australia 6169
Tel: 08 9414 7949
www.littlepacksdistribution.com.au

Reed Craft Supplies
PO Box 181
West Heidelberg
Victoria 3081
Tel: 3 9458 5895
www.reedcraftsupplies.com.au

UK

Craft Creations
Ingersoll House
Delamare Road
Cheshunt
Hertfordshire
EN8 9HD
Tel: 01992 781900
www.craftcreations.com

Fred Aldous
37 Lever Street
Manchester
M1 1LW
Tel: 08707 517 301
www.fredaldous.co.uk

Hobbicraft
40 Woodhouse Lane
Leeds
LS2 8LX
Tel: 0113 2930 636
www.hobbicraft.co.uk

The Craft Barn
9 East Grinstead Road
Lingfield
Surrey
RH7 6EP
Tel: 01342 836097
www.craftbarn.co.uk

USA

CraftAmerica
498 Dreyfus Road
Berea
KY 4043
Tel: 800 407 5090
www.craftamerica.com

Crafts Etc!
7717 SW 44th Street
Oklahoma City
OK 73179
Tel: 800 888 0321
www.craftsetc.com

Craft King
12750 W. Capitol Dr.
Brookfield
WI 53005
Tel: 262 781 9660
www.craftking.com

National ArtCraft
300 Campus Drive
Aurora
OH 44202
Tel: 888 937 2723
www.nationalartcraft.com

INDEX

For a complete catalogue or to place an order, contact:
GMC Publications Ltd, Castle Place, 166 High Street, Lewes, East Sussex, BN7 1XU United Kingdom
Tel: 01273 488005 Fax: 01273 402866
Website: www.thegmcgroup.com
Orders by credit card are accepted